WHAT'S iN A... CACTUS?

Tracy Nelson Maurer

Rourke
Educational Media

rourkeeducationalmedia.com

www.rourkeeducationalmedia.com

Photo credits: Cover © Four Oaks; Page 3 © EuToch; Page 4 © Flnur; Page 5 © Daniel Zuckerkandel; Page 6 © Daniel Zuckerkandel; Page 7 © noolwlee; Page 8 © Picstudio; Page 9 © risteski goce; Page 10 © Crabbiroader; Page 11 © Voyagerix; Page 12 © Voyagerix; Page 13 © Braam Collins; Page 14 © Orangeline; Page 15 © Hannamariah; Page 16 © Thomas Barrat; Page 17 © Stasys Eidiejus; Page 18 © Ken Bosma, Nathan Chor; Page 19 © GRISHA; Page 20 © ZouZou; Page 21 © Brooke Whatnall, Lijuan Guo, fivespots; Page 22 © Ken Bosma, Nathan Chor, Crabbiroader, Thomas Barrat; Page 23 © Voyagerix, Orangeline, Picstudio

Editor: Jeanne Sturm

Cover and page design by Nicola Stratford, Blue Door Publishing

Library of Congress Cataloging-in-Publication Data

Maurer, Tracy, 1965-
 Cactus / Tracy Nelson Maurer.
    p. cm. -- (What's in a...?)
 Includes bibliographical references and index.
 ISBN 978-1-61590-282-8 (alk. paper)
 ISBN 978-1-61590-521-8 (soft cover)
 1. Cactus--Juvenile literature. I. Title.
 QK495.C11M3816 2011
 583'.56--dc22
                              2010009255

Also Available as:
ROURKE'S
e-Books

Rourke Educational Media
Printed in the United States of America,
North Mankato, Minnesota

Rourke
Educational Media

rourkeeducationalmedia.com

customerservice@rourkeeducationalmedia.com • PO Box 643328 Vero Beach, Florida 32964

A cactus is a prickly
plant full of life.

Can you guess what's in a cactus?

4

What pecks a hole for
a nest in a cactus?

5

A bird.

What climbs up a
cactus to hunt?

A **lizard.**

What howls in the
shadow of a cactus?

A **coyote.**

What blooms beside the sharp needles?

A **flower.**

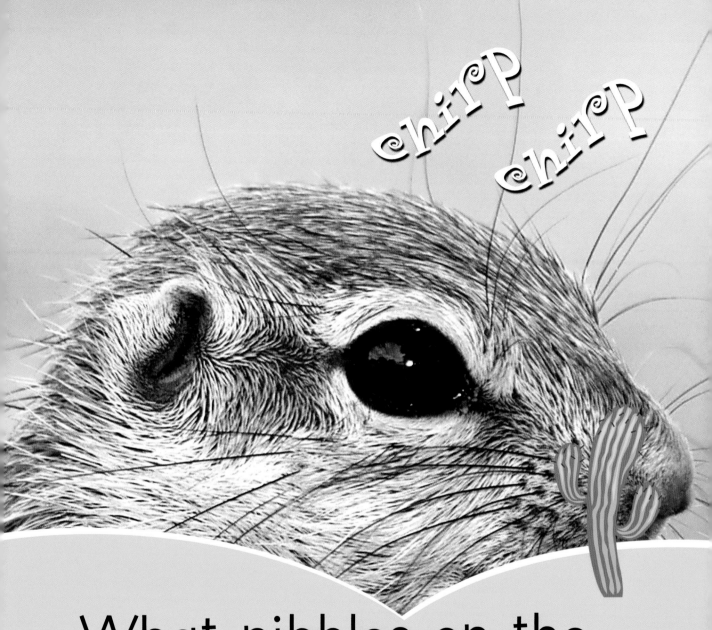

What nibbles on the green cactus parts?

13

A **desert ground** squirrel.

What flutters by to
drink nectar?

A **butterfly.**

What night flier visits the cactus flowers?

A **bat.**

18

mmmm

What drinks juice made from cactus sap?

Me!

20

What else could *you* see in a cactus?

Picture Glossary

bat (BAT): A bat is a small, flying mammal that mostly feeds at night. The bat finds its way by making squeaking sounds that echo off nearby objects.

coyote (kye-OH-tee): The coyote eats nearly any small animal or insect. This helps it survive in many habitats, from deserts to cities.

butterfly (BUT-er-fly): A butterfly uses its feet to smell for the sweet flower juice called nectar.

flower (FLOU-er): Flowers usually bloom on cactus plants between February and April. The bright colors and sweet nectar attract insects, birds, and bats.

desert ground squirrel (DEZ-ert GROUND SKWERL-ul): A desert ground squirrel lives in a burrow dug with its sharp claws. This rodent eats many kinds of plants.

lizard (LIZ-urd): A lizard is a cold-blooded reptile. It warms its body on sunny rocks, sand dunes, or plants as it rests and watches for prey.

Index

Websites

www.kids.nationalgeographic.com

www.eol.org/

www.inaturalist.org/taxa

About The Author

Tracy Nelson Maurer likes to explore the area near Minneapolis, Minnesota, where she lives with her husband and two children. She holds an MFA in Writing for Children & Young Adults from Hamline University.

Meet The Author!
www.meetREMauthors.com